FAITH
THE COW

WRITTEN BY SUSAN BAME HOOVER
ILLUSTRATED BY MAGGIE SYKORA

faithQuest™ ◆ Brethren Press™

Dan West (1893-1971) was the genius behind Heifer Project International. Heifer Project began as a project of the Church of the Brethren in 1944 to alleviate hunger and poverty. It continues today as an ecumenical nonprofit organization with many member agencies. HPI helps struggling families become self-sufficient, supplying them with farm animals, training and technical help. Recipients agree to share know-how with others and to pass on the offspring of their livestock to others in their community, thus multiplying the gift.

17 16 15 14 13   12 11 10 9 8

Library of Congress Cataloging-in-Publication Data

Hoover, Susan Bame, 1957-
        Faith the cow / Susan Bame Hoover ; Maggie Sykora, illustrator.
            p.   cm.
        ISBN 0-87178-229-4

        1. Heifer Project-Juvenile literature. 2. Agricultural assistance-Juvenile literature. 3. Milk programs-Juvenile literature. 4. Food relief-Juvenile literature. [1. Heifer Project. 2. Food relief.] I. Sykora, Maggie, 1955-2000-ill. II. Title.
SF140.L59H444   1995   94-40763
363.8'83—dc20

Manufactured in the United States

Give a man a fish,
       he can eat for a day.
Teach a man to fish,
       he can eat for a lifetime.

—Old proverb

In loving memory of Grandma,
Amanda Smith Bame,
who had a soft lap,
open arms,
and the world's best stories.

—S.B.H.

To my mother,
Peggy Seaton,
whose loving encouragement
taught me how to fish.

—M.S.

This is a story of Faith.

Faith was a young Guernsey cow—a heifer.
Faith was a special Guernsey heifer.
     She had a job to do.

Faith was a heifer with a mission.

Dan West loved peace.
Dan West hated war.

Dan West was ordered to serve in the army. But when he told
the officer that he wouldn't carry a gun and he couldn't kill,
the army sent Dan West home. Dan West knew there was
a better way to settle disagreements.

Once there was a war in Spain.

Instead of fighting, Dan West went to Spain to hand out
food and supplies to families who lost everything in the war.

He felt sad for people who lived where soldiers fought.
He felt sad for the children who had no milk to drink.
They had no milk to drink in Spain
because the soldiers killed the cows.

He felt sad for the mothers,
fathers, daughters, sons, and
grandparents who died in
the fighting.

When Dan West looked at the children in Spain, he thought of his roly-poly babies at home, Joel and Janet, who had plenty to eat.

Dan West thought about his childhood
home in Ohio where Guernsey cows filled big red barns.

Dan West had an idea. He dreamed of giving
one milk cow to a starving family.
   One cow could feed many children.
      One cow could have many babies.
      These calves could feed even more families.

But where would Dan West get a cow? He wasn't a farmer.
Where would he get a ship to carry the cow? He wasn't a sailor.
How would he take care of the cow while she sailed across the ocean?
    He wasn't an animal doctor.

Just one man, just one cow? That just wouldn't be enough.
So Dan West began to look for people who could
help him make his dream come true.

Dan West told a group of farmers in his church about the starving children in the world. When Dan West finished, Virgil Mock stood up.

Virgil Mock said,

Dan West said, "I have faith, Virgil. I believe God is telling us to help. We need to send heifers to give milk for the children. But I can't do it by myself. I need help."

Virgil Mock said again,

Dan West said, "I do have faith, Virgil. I trust God to make my dream come true, even though it seems impossible."

Virgil Mock said,

"No, Dan West. I mean have *Faith*.
Faith is my Guernsey cow."

Then another farmer, whose red barn was full of
Guernsey cows, gave a heifer to Dan West. Then another
farmer gave a heifer, and another, until the farmers had
given Dan West seventeen cows.

The first three heifers the farmers gave to Dan West were named

Faith,

Hope,

and Charity.

Faith and sixteen other heifers came to church one Sunday.
The pastor prayed over the cows, laid his hands on them and blessed them,
and sent them out into the world to help families.

Faith was no longer just one heifer with a mission.
Now there were seventeen heifers with a mission!

Faith, the Guernsey cow, rode to Mobile, Alabama,
in the back of a big truck.

Then she sailed to the island of Puerto Rico, where she found a happy home.

There were ten children in Faith's new family.
They loved their cow and learned to take good care of her.
It was the children's job to feed Faith, protect her, and keep her clean.

Faith took good care of her new family, too.
She gave the children lots of milk.

The whole family was very happy. For the first time ever, they owned something valuable—a cow! And no one was hungry.

Soon Faith had a calf. That first calf made the family very proud. Now they could help someone else just as Dan West helped them.

They gave the calf to a neighbor family. The neighbors needed help, too.

Faith's family taught the neighbors how to take good care of the new calf. Someday, that calf would feed another family.

Dan West and the farmers called their plan "Heifer Project." It was easier to say "Heifer Project" than to say

A-group-of-farmers-who-give-their-young-cows-to-Dan-West-so-he-can-send-them-around-the-world-to-help-feed-hungry-children.

Heifer Project began to send more and more animals to feed people all over the world.

Rabbits were sent.

Goats, chickens, and honeybees were sent.

Draft horses, sheep, and pigs were sent.

Ducks, geese, and fish were sent.

Can just one person
make a difference?
Can just one
person with
an idea
help feed
hungry
children
all
around
the
world?

Can
just
one
person
make
the world
a better place?

One person can make a difference— if that person has a little ...

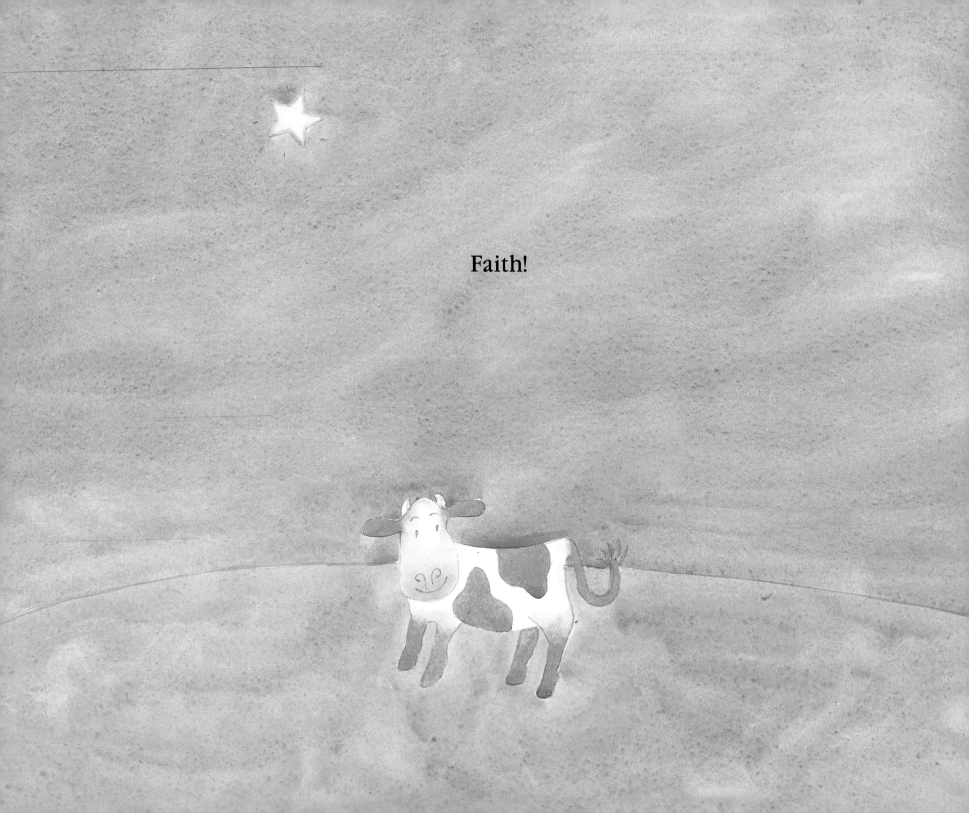

Faith!